The Power of
THANKSGIVING

Robert Strand

E✦ergreen
PRESS

ISBN 1-58169-054-1
For Worldwide Distribution
Printed in U.S.A.

Evergreen Press
P.O. Box 91011 • Mobile, AL 36691
800-367-8203

TABLE OF CONTENTS

DEDICATION

Dedicated to Donna Marie,
a wonderful wife, mother, and grandmother
who has taught all of us who are part of her family
how to live a life filled with thanksgiving.
Her most often repeated prayer are the words,
"Thank you, thank you, thank you,
thank you, Lord!"

Chapter 1

THE TASTE BERRY

In Africa there's a fruit called the "taste berry," so-called because it changes a person's taste buds in such a way that everything eaten after it tastes sweet. Even bitter foods, if consumed within several hours after a taste berry, are quite delicious.

Giving thanks is the "taste berry" of Christianity. When our hearts are filled with gratitude, nothing that comes our way will be unpalatable to us. Those whose lifestyle is marked by thanksgiving will enjoy a sweetness of life unparalleled by any other.

The phrase, "with thanksgiving," is one of the primary ways the Bible refers to positive communication. Time and again, we are told to pray, give praise, express love, do our positive deeds, and offer adoration, all "with thanksgiving." By their very nature, these activities are positive. They cause us to focus on God—who He is, what He has done, what He is doing, and what He will do. This helps us to resist the ever present temptation to focus on ourselves.

Thanksgiving also brings humility, which is the saving grace that can preserve our society. Learning to say "thank you" may seem like such an *easy* thing, but it is never a *little* thing! Even the Lord of the universe wants to be thanked: "Through Jesus, therefore, let us continually offer to God a sacrifice of praise…the fruit of lips that confess his name. And do not forget to do good and to share with others, for with such sacrifices God is pleased" (Hebrews 13:15-16).

When parents teach their children to be grateful, they build protection against moral erosion into their lives. One young son was taught to bring everything to the Lord in prayer. When called upon to give the blessing at dinner time, he invariably added at the end of his prayer, "And Lord, please bless all our needs. Thank you, in Jesus' name."

The atmosphere of heaven itself is one of thanksgiving and praise. So thanksgiving can literally create a bit of heaven in your home when your children begin to automatically thank God for His blessings. It will do the same in your office or workplace, in society, and in your church.

Thanksgiving cleanses. It's a cathartic for the soul. It's an expression of dependence on God! A dependent person never feels proud in an unhealthy sense of the word. On the other hand, a proud person does not really *petition* God—he simply *informs* God so that he can take delivery on the merchandise.

But God's way is so different: "Do not be anxious about anything, but in everything, by prayer and petition, with thanksgiving, present your requests to God" (Philippians 4:6). This type of prayer flushes negativity out of the mind and soul and reestablishes our priorities.

There's a pastor I know in the deep South who doesn't have a single hair on his head. Baldness can be one of life's slightly embarrassing situations and has made him the object of good-natured teasing. His colleagues call him "Mister Clean." At a preachers' meeting one day, he stood to share a testimony and ended with, "I thank God for two perfectly good eyebrows!"

Everyone joined in warm laughter. Here was a man who definitely lived his life with thanksgiving and not complaint! Thanksgiving purges the negative, the murmuring, the complaining, the whining—even about the little things—from our lives. Giving thanks is truly an effective taste berry for daily living!

(Hebrews 13:15-16; Philippians 4:6;
2 Corinthians 5:17)

POWER POINT: Is there a taste berry in your life? Does life seem sweet or do you face every day with some degree of bitterness? Take this test periodically: When you pass a mirror or see your reflection in a store window, are you smiling or frowning? Try finding something about your circumstances for which you can be grateful and let it bring a smile to your face. Practice this several times a day, and you'll soon be surprised how differently everything seems.

Chapter 2

A MAGNET FOR BLESSINGS

If one should give me a dish of sand and tell me there were particles of iron in it, I might look for them with my eyes and search for them with my clumsy fingers and be unable to detect them; but let me take a magnet and sweep through it and it would draw to itself the almost invisible particles by the mere power of attraction.

The unthankful heart, like my finger in the sand, discovers no mercies; but let the thankful heart sweep through the day and as the magnet finds iron, so it will find, in every hour, some heavenly blessings, only the iron in God's sand is gold! —*Henry Ward Beecher*

Do you know people who have cultivated the habit of being thankful? They are amazing people who, no matter what happens, seem to be able to

5

walk in peace and have a measure of joy. They have no doubt found the priceless "gold" that thankfulness has uncovered in their life.

The Apostle Paul gives us a key to developing this "stress busting" quality in his letter to the Thessalonians: "Be joyful always; pray continually; give thanks in all circumstances, for this is God's will for you in Christ Jesus" (I Thessalonians 5:16-18).

"No way," you say? "He didn't know what life would be like in the 21st century!" Wait a minute. Do you notice something significant in this verse? It doesn't say "give thanks FOR all circumstances!" It says, "give thanks IN all circumstances." There is a big difference!

Matthew Henry, the noted Bible scholar, was once accosted by thieves, who robbed him of all the money he had on him. Following this experience, he wrote these words in his diary: "Let me be thankful first, because I was never robbed before; second, although they took my billfold, they did not take my life; third, because, although they took my all, it was not much; and fourth, because it was I who was robbed, not I who robbed." Henry was a man who obviously had learned how to "give thanks IN all circumstances!" That's how this "giving thanks *in*" business works in real life.

Your circumstances may be out of your control, but whether or not you are thankful in the midst of them is under your control. Thankfulness is a habit that must be cultivated if you really want to enjoy life. According to experts, in order to develop a habit, you must repeat it at least 21 times. Habits also require constant attention and self-control, but once the gold is uncovered in your life, you'll be rich beyond measure!

(I Thessalonians 5:16-18)

⚡ POWER POINT: Why not make the decision to be thankful IN all things for the next 21 days? Post reminders everywhere—on your dresser mirror, on the refrigerator door, or at your desk, for example—so that you will remember to look for things all day long in which to give thanks.

Chapter 3

A Gift of Thanks

Living with a grateful heart is quite rare today, but it should be a common, everyday grace. The late W.L. Stidger shared about how one of his English teachers had gone out of her way to interest him in the writings of the poet Tennyson. Her concern for William had definitely made a difference in his life and was something he had never forgotten.

After he graduated, every Thanksgiving he wrote to people who had influenced him significantly over the years. One year, he wrote this English teacher a simple letter of appreciation. Not long afterward, he received this encouraging reply:

"My Dear Willie: I am an old lady in my eighties now. I am ill, and I cannot leave my room. Your letter came like a ray of bright sun, illuminating my dark day and my even darker life. You will be interested to know that, after 50 years of teaching, yours was the first letter of thanks I ever received from a former student. You lifted the clouds for me." There's power in bestowing a gift of thanks!

"Thanksgiving" to most of us is a celebration on the fourth Thursday of November each year. But it really goes much beyond the turkey and dressing rituals. As we break it down, "thanks" is a simple, yet profound expression of gratitude, appreciation, or acknowledgment. "Giving" is an act, a presentation of a gift. In "thanksgiving" we do the act of expressing our gratitude. It can be a celebration—public or private.

The Bible is filled with injunctions to be thankful and express our thanks. Throughout Psalms, David wrote song after song containing expressions of thanks to the Lord. The New Testament is also full of this same encouragement. Let's consider: "Do not be anxious about anything, but in everything, by prayer and petition, with thanksgiving, present your requests to God" (Philippians 4:6).

"So then just as you received Christ Jesus as Lord, continue to live in Him, rooted and built up in Him, strengthened in the faith as you were taught, and overflowing with thankfulness" (Colossians 2:6-7).

"I urge, then, first of all, that requests, prayers, intercession and thanksgiving be made for everyone…" (I Timothy 2:1).

"By Him therefore let us offer the sacrifice of praise to God continually, that is, the fruit of our lips giving thanks to his name" (Hebrews 13:15, KJV).

With these numerous commands from the Word of God, it's obvious how much God values an offering of thanks. It's to be much more than a yearly celebration; it's to be a lifestyle. It's to be a grace practiced *all* the time in *all* kinds of circumstances. It's a discipline to be learned, a self-control to exercise, a mind-set to cultivate, a habit to create, a lifestyle to embrace!

Thanksgiving is to be offered to God as well as to others. Overflowing with thanks no matter what the circumstances is a beautiful example of living the Christian life.

In 1636, in the midst of the darkness of the "Thirty Years' War," there was a German pastor, Martin Rinkart, who was reported to have conducted funeral services for more than 5,000 of his parishioners in one year, an average of 15 per day. His parish was ravaged by war, death, disease, and economic disaster.

In the very heart of that darkness, with the cries of fear just outside his window, he sat down and penned this table grace for his children. In fact you may have sung it lately:

> Now thank we all our God
> With heart and hands and voices;
> Who wondrous things hath done,
> In whom his world rejoices.
> Who, from our mother's arms,
> Hath led us on our way

With countless gifts of love
And still is ours today.

Here was a man who knew that thanksgiving springs out of our relationship with God and not from outward circumstances.

(Colossians 2:6-7; I Timothy 2:1; Hebrews 13:15)

POWER POINT: Think about the people who have made a difference in your life, especially when you were younger. Attempt to contact one of them by phone, e-mail, or letter. Tell them exactly how they were a particular blessing to you and helped to make you what you are today.

Chapter 4

SUNRISES AND FLOWERS

What if...tomorrow morning, the sun doesn't rise? Alarm clocks all over town would go off at 6:00 AM, 7:00 AM, 8:00 AM...but there would be no light! No birds would be singing. The only sounds would be the hoot of the owl and the swoop of the bat, flying through the dark sky.

Noon would come—yet still no light! Then, all afternoon long, more hours of darkness. Weeping and panic would sweep all across the land. Churches would be filled with kneeling people, pleading for help from above. There would be no sleep that night. Everyone would periodically peer out their windows, hoping to see a faint glimmer of light.

The next morning, millions of eager, tear-stained faces would be turned toward the east. When the sky finally began to redden and then glow with golden light, there would be a great shout of joy! Bells would toll in church steeples everywhere. People would be dancing in the streets, intense joy written on their faces. Millions would be eager to thank God. And for what? A simple sunrise! How many mornings have we thanked God for that blessing?

It's a wonderful world of splendor in which we live! How can anyone live in this world and not be awed by it? How can we take it for granted? How can we snivel, sneer, boast, and brag when creation itself is infinitely more valuable than anything we could accomplish? "For since the creation of the world God's invisible qualities...his eternal power and divine nature...have been clearly seen, being understood from what has been made, so that men are without excuse" (Romans 1:20).

While thanksgiving opens our eyes to eternity, thanklessness closes our eyes to it. It makes only the present and visible real and causes us to say, "I do not believe in the eternal."

There are no miracles nor beauty for thankless people. They refuse to believe in a God who could take a handful of clay, deposit it deep into the earth, subject it to great heat and pressure, and create a beautiful amethyst! They ignore the Creator who took a handful of carbon, planted it deep into the hot bowels of the earth, pressed it with rocks and mountains, and transformed it into a beautiful diamond. Neither of these creative wonders contain a message for thankless people. Paul the Apostle says such people have "exchanged the truth of God for a lie" (Romans 1:25a).

The truth is that the Creator who changes clay

into amethysts and carbon into diamonds also transforms the souls of men and women. The same God performs these bigger miracles.

The Bible is very concerned about unthankful people. In an "autopsy" on a former generation, the Apostle Paul declares that one of the root causes of that generation's failure was thanklessness. "For although they knew God, they neither glorified him as God nor gave thanks to him, but their thinking became futile and their foolish hearts were darkened" (Romans 1:21). Out of unthankfulness came such things as idolatry, degeneracy, apostasy, perversion, violence, delinquency, and lawlessness. When we cease to humbly acknowledge God's goodness, we open the floodgates to all kinds of wickedness. (You can read the context in Romans 1:1-2:16.)

Why are we so unthankful? Perhaps we allow the constancy of God's blessings and benefits to kill our gratitude. We begin to take them for granted, instead of being thankful to Him.

His many blessings should make us cry out to Him:

> BLESS the LORD, O my soul; And all that is within me, bless His holy name! Bless the LORD, O my soul, And forget not all His benefits:
> WHO forgives all your iniquities,
> WHO heals all your diseases,
> WHO redeems your life from destruction,

WHO crowns you with lovingkindness and
    tender mercies,
WHO satisfies your mouth with good things,
So that your youth is renewed like the eagle's.
                  (Psalm 103:1-5 NKJV).

I know that God can take your life—even if it
seems to be drab and useless—and change it into a
new creation! "Therefore, if anyone is in Christ, he
is a new creation; the old has gone, the new has
come!" (II Corinthians 5:17).

Thank Him for Calvary! Thank Him for eternity! Thank Him for hope that is eternal! There is a
better way!

(Romans 1:20-21; Psalm 103:1-5)

POWER POINT: Go for a walk this evening
and take a good look around you at God's magnificent creation. When you get back home, spend some
time thanking God for all the wonders that He has
given to mankind.

Chapter 5

THE ART
OF THANKFULNESS

"Every morning I give thanks for all the wonderful things in my life," declared a young man enthusiastically to me. He continued, "And do you know something? It's strange…but the more I give thanks, the more I have reason to be thankful. I've discovered that blessings just continue to pile up on me, one after another, like nobody's business."

What an insightful young man! He sure captured my interest. In his remarks he had stated a basic law of the universe: THE MORE YOU PRACTICE THE ART OF THANKFULNESS, THE MORE YOU HAVE TO BE THANKFUL FOR!

This is a fact. Thankfulness tends to reproduce in kind, as does anything else. It reverses the ebb of good things away from you and sets in motion a tide of good things flowing back to you. An attitude of gratitude revitalizes your mental processes by activating other positive attitudes which, in turn, stimulate your creativity and produce amazing results.

This kind of attitude helps you focus so you will work better, think better, get along with people better, and be able to use your abilities to their fullest extent. This attitude, which you can cultivate, will allow you to function more effectively in every aspect of your life!

Too many people are plagued by concentrating on the difficulties and problems in their life. This type of wrong thinking will inevitably produce bad results. Right thinking produces good fruit. It's that old saying in computer programming: GIGO. "Garbage in equals garbage out."

Your life *can be changed* by consistently practicing the art of thankfulness. How? Start each day by considering how many things you can be thankful for. Repeat them over and over to yourself. Declare them to God. Share them with your spouse. Mention them to your fellow workers. You will be amazed at what begins to happen.

This can be the beginning of a huge turnaround in your mind and lifestyle. It's a powerful habit that yields abundant life.

None of us should ever be too busy to be thankful. It takes just a few seconds to express gratitude by simply offering a heart-warming "thank you."

Theodore Roosevelt probably lived as hectic

and hurried a life as any American before or since. In the heat of political campaigning, it would have been so easy for him to ignore the feelings of others. However, every time he left his private train, he stopped and thanked the engineer and fireman for a safe and comfortable trip. It took only a few seconds, but he had made two more friends for the rest of his life.

"Good politics," you may be thinking. Not only that…but good living, too! Think about it…aren't relationships the foundation for happy living?

An elderly woman never left an airplane without thanking the captain and crew. A small gesture…perhaps. But what captain or crew member is so jaded that an acknowledgement of their service would be refused? Even total strangers can be blessed with a nod of your head, a gesture of your hand, a grateful look, and a happy "thank you." It can happen anywhere…on a crowded commuter bus, at a packed lunch counter, in the quiet of a church service, or waiting in line at a checkout counter. In fact, you can spread blessing just about everywhere if your heart is saying, "Thank you!"

In a manner of speaking, this world is an expression of God's will. It's a harmonious creation with predictable days and nights, seasons of warmth and cold, clouds which deposit life-sustaining rain along with the sun which provides warmth to all living things…all working together. Why couldn't we, as humans, created in the image of God, also flow in warm, wonderful relationships which are held together by the common courtesy of thankfulness?

(Psalm 103:1)

POWER POINT: Try this simple experiment: Select an area of your life that's not going well. Then spend about 15-30 minutes considering this area of your life in light of your knowledge of God and prayer. Remind yourself that this difficult area of your life must also come under the law of thankfulness. Explore the truth of it from God's perspective. Give thanks for it or at least some part of it and then put it aside. Repeat this procedure tomorrow and every day thereafter until your gratitude becomes genuine and you begin to see a change in this area of your life.

Chapter 6

WHY THANKSGIVING IS SO RARE

Thanksgiving is a very simple thing...as a matter of fact, it is based on one important ingredient. It's something that's compatible with any kind of life—*your* life, for example. If you take this ingredient and add it to your current circumstances, you'll experience the reality of thanksgiving. What is it? *Contentment!* It's what God calls a life lived in thanksgiving. "But godliness with contentment is great gain. For we brought nothing into the world, and we can take nothing out of it. But if we have food and clothing, we will be content with that" (I Timothy 6:6-8). Powerful! Awesome! Simple? Yes.

Will you agree with me that contentment is rare, extremely rare? Name the people you know who are content, and you'll discover it's a very short list. Discontentment is shared by the rich and poor alike. You'd think the rich would be content, but often they experience it the least. How much does it take to make people content? It always seems to be just a little bit more!

How much is enough? The Russian author, Leo Tolstoy, tells the story of a rich peasant who was never satisfied. He always wanted more and more. He heard of a wonderful chance to get more land. For 1,000 rubles he could have as much land as he could walk around in one day. The only stipulation was that he had to make it back to the starting point by sundown or he would lose it all.

He arose early and set out. He walked farther and farther, thinking he could get just a little more land if he kept on going. He had gone very far when he realized he must walk very fast if he was to get back in time to claim the land. As the sun sank lower in the sky, he quickened his pace. He began to run. As he got within sight of the starting point, he exerted his last ounce of energy, lunged over the finish line, and collapsed on the ground. A trickle of blood seeped from his mouth, and he lay dead. His servant took a spade and dug a grave. He made it just long enough and just wide enough and buried him. Tolstoy concluded his story, "Six feet from his head to his heels was all he needed."

Let's pause right here and make a personal assessment. Can you honestly say, "I am overwhelmed by thanksgiving to God?" Would you like to be able to say that? Let me share two steps you can take toward experiencing contentment.

First: MAKE A MODEST APPRAISAL OF YOUR PHYSICAL NEEDS. If you have food, clothing, and shelter, you should be content. Right? In reality, there is nothing that contradicts the spirit of this age more than contentment with your present situation. Unfortunately, this age is one in which our passionate desire for things is inflamed into a fever pitch! Everywhere we look, this passion for more is encouraged. Ours is a soft, fat, luxurious age, and many grown-ups are spoiled children as far as their wants are concerned. We never seem to be satisfied!

The principle that drives our society is simply this: MORE, MORE, and MORE! It's shouted at us from all sides—we need more money, more cars, more toys, more entertainment, more play time.

Yes, I know that there are some people in our society who have been deprived of many of the basics. They live in an entirely different situation than most of us. What I'm talking about are the greed, avarice, and covetousness that smolders in most of our bosoms without justification. No matter how much we have, this world of ours keeps urging us to try to get more!

When you step into the world of the Bible, it's like stepping onto another planet. The Bible appraises our physical needs differently. Food and clothing—if you have these, you have enough. Ouch…that hurts. In the greatest prayer of all time,

Jesus taught us to pray: "Give us this day our daily bread…"

The second step toward contentment: UNDER-STAND THAT ALL THE MATERIAL THINGS THAT MAKE US HAPPY ARE RELATIVELY UNIMPORTANT. At best, every "thing" we possess is temporary! How, then, is it possible to really be content with material things? So the larger question is: How can we become content with our basic ne-cessities and rid ourselves of this inordinate love for money and things?

Honestly, I don't think there is any earthly way to get rid of these desires by ourselves! But God…and I'm so grateful for that simple phrase… But God can show us, God can help us. The secret is in applying the written Word of God to the greedy soul.

When you find yourself green with envy of the rich, with a desire for more money so real you can taste it, take a dose of the Word. Particularly read Psalm 49:

> *Hear this, all you peoples; listen, all who live in this world…. No man can redeem the life of an-other or give to God ransom for him—the ransom for a life is costly, no payment is ever enough…. But man, despite his riches, does not endure; he is like the beasts that perish. This is the fate of those who trust in themselves…. Do not be overawed when a man grows rich, when the splendor of his*

house increases; *for he will take nothing with him when he dies. A man who has riches without understanding is like the beasts that perish* (Psalm 49:1,7-8,12-13,16-17,20).

How's that for a dose of reality? We'll have to let go of it all when we die! Have you ever seen a hearse with a U-Haul® trailer behind it? After Howard Hughes had died, many asked the question: "How much money did he leave?" You're right…he left it all!

IF YOU REALLY WANT TO BE CONTENT, you must believe that God is in charge of your life and that He will take care of you tomorrow and the next day and all the tomorrows which follow. Now that's a powerful life!

(Psalm 49:1-20)

⚡ POWER POINT: If you could take only one of your personal possessions with you into heaven, what would it be and why?

Chapter 7

RELEASE GOD'S POWER

Giving thanks is a biblical way to release the power of God. When Jesus fed the 5000 on a hillside, note He did not pray for the multiplication miracle...*He merely gave thanks!* (See John 6:11.) This thanks, by itself, released a divine power that turned the elements of the little boy's humble meal into an over-abundant one for 5,000 men, to say nothing of the women and children present!

Likewise, when Jesus stood before the tomb of Lazarus, He didn't pray a prayer of petition. He simply thanked the Father that He always heard Him (see John 11:41-42). This released the power needed to call forth from the tomb a man who had been dead four days!

Giving thanks is the will of God in *any* and *all* situations! Understanding this key principle will have a direct bearing on how we pray.

In one of his prayer journals, John Wesley focuses on three words: EVERYTHING IN PRAYER. About these words, Wesley wrote: "I am persuaded that God does everything by prayer and nothing without it." Talk about truth with a punch to it. He had focused on the verse from the Bible that says, "Be anxious for nothing; but in everything by prayer and supplication *with thanksgiving* let your requests be made known unto God" (Philippians 4:6 KJV, emphasis added).

There is no higher ministry in the Christian life than prayer. It is both a science, which must be studied, and an art, which needs to be cultivated. The relationship of prayer to the Christian lifestyle can be compared to a transformer and the electrical service we use. Our house may be wired properly, but if it isn't connected to the transformer, nothing happens. Too many churches are like this. They have all the programs and activities in place, but they lack supernatural power, which can only come through prayer.

When certain principles are consistently practiced, they will undergird a successful prayer discipline. One of these principles is the importance of RIGHT ACCESS. God's requirement for this is stated in Psalm 100:4-5: "Enter his gates with thanksgiving and his courts with praise; give thanks to him and praise his name. For the Lord is good and his love endures forever; his faithfulness continues through all generations." It's only as we approach God in this manner that we will have access into His presence.

Confronted with this principle, we are sometimes tempted to look at our situation and think,

"What do I have to thank God for?" There may *seem* to be nothing for which you can express thanks. But the Psalmist has given us at least three reasons to thank and praise that are NOT affected by our current circumstances: First, the Lord is good! Second, His love endures forever! And third, His faithfulness continues throughout all generations! All three of these reasons are eternal, unchanging facts. If we really believe these truths, then we have no alternative but to praise God for them continually!

If we omit thanksgiving and praise, we will be like the nine lepers who did not return to praise the Lord for their healing (see Luke 17:11-19). The original Greek language indicates that all 10 lepers were healed *physically*, but only the one who returned to give thanks was also healed *spiritually*! Returning to give thanks set an eternal seal upon him. This is one way to insure that our blessings from God are eternal!

The second principle that is important to successful prayer is we must pray ACCORDING TO GOD'S WORD. When you pray, don't you want to do it according to His will and Word? The Apostle John tells us, "If we ask anything according to His [God's] will, he hears us...whatever we ask...we know that we have what we asked of him" (I John 5:14-15).

The critical issue in prayer always is to pray according to God's will. How can we be sure we are

doing this? One of the best ways is by always beginning prayer with thanksgiving and praise! When we
focus on God and His love for us, it will keep us focused on what is truly important!

Therefore, when you petition, when you pray,
when you approach God...don't omit your grateful
offering of thanksgiving and praise!

(Philippians 4:6; Psalm 100:4-5; I John 5:14-15)

⚡ POWER POINT: Do you begin praying with
thanks or do you often find yourself complaining?
Even if you don't *feel* thankful, go ahead and verbally
thank God for what He's *going to do* in answer to your
prayer!

Chapter 8

FROM DISASTER TO DOXOLOGY

The decade of the 1660s in England was filled with disaster. The plague in 1665 made its way through the city of London, leaving more than 70,000 dead. A year later, a disastrous fire destroyed much of the heart of that city. The prophets of doom and gloom predicted that London and England would never recover.

During all of this pain and difficulty, a godly Christian man, Bishop Thomas Ken, kept encouraging the people that he could still see the light of God's purpose and presence even through the tough times they were experiencing then.

One night he felt inspired to write a song which would give testimony to his conviction that God was still sovereign and most worthy of thanksgiving and praise. The following four lines have been one of the most frequently sung words of any known song for more than 300 years!

Praise God from whom all blessings flow,
Praise Him all creatures here below,
Praise Him above ye heavenly host.
Praise Father, Son, and Holy Ghost!

Praise is derived from the Latin word, *preisier,* which means "to prize." Therefore, praise is an expression of approval, a worship, and a valuation of that which has worth. To praise is to prize, to glorify the one worthy of glory. To the degree that something or someone is worthy of glory and honor, to that degree praise is due.

One day a choir was rehearsing Handel's "Messiah." They were being led by the great conductor Reichel, and this was their last rehearsal. The soprano soloist came to the last refrain of "I Know That My Redeemer Liveth" and sang it with perfect technique. When she finished, Reichel stopped the orchestra. The choir expected praise of the soloist for her perfect rendition. But he didn't give it to her! He looked down at her from his podium and asked, "Oh, my daughter, do you *know Him*? Do you really know Him as your Redeemer?"

Shattered by his question, the soloist, who was a devout Christian, stammered, "Yes...yes, Mr. Reichel, I DO know Him! He IS my Redeemer!"

In almost a shout, the great conductor cried, "THEN SING IT! Sing it so that I will know!" He signaled the orchestra to begin the section once again.

Now, oblivious to all the techniques she had learned and knowing that she had not fully praised the Lord the first time, the soprano poured out her soul in the magnificence of her trained voice. Her praise soared on the emotion of her singing: "I KNOW THAT MY REDEEMER LIVETH!"

The choir and orchestra burst into applause when she finished. Reichel turned to her, eyes gleaming with tears: "Oh, my dear, you DO know Him, for you have just told me!"

To know Him is to praise Him! To know Him is to offer fervent thanksgiving to Him!

(Job 19:25)

⚡ POWER POINT: This week tell someone outside your family or church what you're thankful for and why.

Chapter 9
WHY I AM THANKFUL

The following piece was written by a 16-year-old Jewish refugee who had managed to immigrate to the United States following the persecution of the Jews in Germany during WWII:

"I am thankful that I live in a land where everyone may salute the same flag.

"I am thankful that I live in a land where, regardless of race, everyone may take part in national ceremonies.

"I am thankful that I live in a land where the future seems bright and hopeful, rather than dark and hopeless.

"I am thankful that I live in a land where the youth of all races have a tomorrow, rather than in my native land where the youth of the race is without a tomorrow.

"I am thankful that I am happy and free!"

How many 16-year-olds do you know who have this kind of attitude? Unfortunately, it is sometimes only when we have lost something that we understand its true significance.

King David was very conscious of having received abundant mercies from the Lord; in fact, he acknowledged that everything he possessed had come from God. He also felt a responsibility to express his thankfulness to God for all His many benefits and did so through his many psalms. He danced before the Lord with such abandon that his wife was embarrassed because she didn't have the same heart of thankfulness toward God. David continually sought to find ways to express an appropriate response to God's mercy and love.

What is an appropriate standard of thankfulness to God against which we should be measured? Okay...good question. More specifically, when should we give thanks; how can we tangibly make our thankfulness known; and when have we given enough? The average Jew of Jesus' day would probably have responded: "by giving the tithe" or 10 percent of the increase. Others may have replied, "by going one mile to help another." But there were biblical characters who raised this standard!

Zacchaeus, the best known short man of the Bible, adopted a higher standard. In response to what the Lord had done on his behalf, he put half of his goods at the disposal of the poor in his area.

Mary Magdalene raised it, too. She broke the alabaster jar of ointment to anoint Jesus. This oil was said to be valued at more than a year's wages. She was not prompted by necessity, nor was she forced to make this offering. She was prompted by her own love and gratitude for what Jesus had done in her life!

An anonymous widow raised the standard even higher. When Jesus and His disciples were in the temple, they observed the giving of offerings. The rich came and presented their gifts, out of their abundance. But when a poor widow gave her last two coins, Jesus declared that she was to be our example because she had given her all. What prompted this sacrifice? We must speculate a bit...but I suspect, that like Mary, she was motivated by her thankfulness to the Lord for His great love for her.

The absolutely finest measure of thanksgiving is gratitude that is followed by some means of tangible expression, prompted by deep love for the recipient! Have we uncovered yet another ingredient of the thankful heart? I believe we have. People who love much also express thanksgiving over and over and, in turn, pass along the blessing to others.

However, monetary giving is not necessarily the best way to express thanksgiving. Shakespeare shares with us a truth about thanksgiving when he called it "the exchequer [treasury] of the poor." The poor may not be able to afford to buy a gift as a means of expressing gratitude, but they can still give something tangible, perhaps even just a thank you note, out of the treasury of their heart. His fervent prayer was, "O Lord, that lends me life, lend me a heart replete with thankfulness!"

It's time we thank God that He has made it possible for us to give something back to Him...the "sacrifice" of praise, the "sacrifice" of thanksgiving!

(John 12:1-8)

POWER POINT: Ask God to help you begin to bless others because you have been so blessed. Then when they attempt to thank you, tell them to "pass it on."

Chapter 10

THE ATTITUDE
OF GRATITUDE

We have so much for which to be grateful, it's
hard to know where to begin. Unfortunately, it
seems to be part of our selfish human nature to take
many good things for granted. After enjoying something that initially was wonderful, special, and fulfilling to us for a few days or weeks, we eventually
become accustomed to it. So what do we do? We
take it for granted! We do this not only with things
but also with people and relationships. If we take
our relationship with our heavenly Father and His
Son for granted, it will definitely have devastating
results.

What should we do? Fight back! Counteract
complacency! Learn to be grateful for the good
things in your life. Make lists...have gratitude
flings...be thankful for little things, big things, every
day things, in fact, everything! Write special "gratitude" notes to remind yourself. Send an e-mail,

write a fax, or create something special in order to express gratitude to someone else!

Let's start right now! Let's begin to appreciate some of the things that are absolutely magnificent, awesome even! Unfortunately, most of us have taken these for granted years ago. What am I talking about? Your God-given senses—sight, touch, taste, smelling and hearing! Then…there's the rest of your body, your brain, your emotions. Add to these your ability to walk, talk, and even use your thumbs. Thumbs? Yes, your thumbs! How would you like to have them amputated? Okay…just try to pick up something from the floor without using them!

Have you ever thanked the Lord for the gift of life? How about the wonderful world of nature which surrounds us? The seasons come and go like clockwork. There is a constancy about God's creation. We need to be grateful it is renewed every morning!

What about your parents, relatives, extended family, neighbors, friends, associates, and the public servants in your life? Ever express gratitude for or to them? The payback is huge.

When you start to notice even a tiny portion of all there is to be grateful for, you'll also discover you don't have time to feel short-changed, hurt or neglected!

The attitude of gratitude is a great, wonderful, exciting, full-of-life feeling! Now…that's real living!

The attitude of gratitude...TRY IT, BEGINNING RIGHT NOW!

(Psalm 139:14-18)

⚡ POWER POINT: Is your giving out of gratitude or done grudgingly? The next time you put something in the offering, thank God for what He's done in your life!

Chapter 11

IT'S THE PROFITABLE THING TO DO

Located in Coffee County in southern Alabama is the town of Enterprise. There they have erected a monument to an insect, honoring the Mexican boll weevil. How can that be? Back in 1895 the boll weevil began to destroy the major crop of the county—cotton. Trying desperately to survive, the farmers decided to diversify and began to plant peanuts. By 1919 the profit from the county's peanut crop was many times greater than what cotton had been at its height.

In that year of prosperity, a fountain and monument were built. The inscription reads: "In profound appreciation of the boll weevil and what it has done as the herald of prosperity. This monument was erected by the citizens of Enterprise, Coffee County, Alabama. Out of a time of struggle and crisis has come new growth and success. Out of diversity has come blessing."

The people of Enterprise could have remained bitter and ungrateful for the soil and climate that enabled the pests to thrive. But instead they decided to pursue a new path which became the *profitable* thing for them to do.

I'm not referring to profitability in the sense that if you thank someone you will be more likely to get something from them. Gratitude promotes profitability in the sense that grateful people are at peace and therefore open to creative ways of doing things. SO…GIVE THANKS!

Jesus is our example in this as in all things. He constantly gave thanks! I freely admit it…it's not always easy to give thanks. For example, here's a difficult question: "How can you thank God for cancer?" At first glance, it seems difficult, if not impossible. I've visited with three different people who have been diagnosed with cancer, and all three have thanked God for His great mercies toward them! Yes…to a Christian, taking gratitude to this extreme is a glorious possibility! To those who are mature in their faith, God's mercies and grace can be found even in the heart of tragedy.

There are times when offering gratitude really becomes "a sacrifice of praise," an offering in the face of tragedy, an expression in the throes of disaster. We can only speculate how precious this kind of thanksgiving is in God's sight.

Thank God those times which stretch our faith

so far don't come all the time. They only visit occa-sionally, thank you, Lord.

We are often put to shame in our thanklessness by people who are less fortunate than us, yet they have learned the secret of giving thanks.

Always and in all circumstances...GIVING THANKS IS THE PROFITABLE THING TO DO!

(Hebrews 13:15-16)

⚡ POWER POINT: Are you struggling with something in your business, in your life? As you think about it, bring it to the Lord with thanksgiving. Tell Him you know He has a purpose for this problem in your life and that you are open to hearing His cre-ative solution.

Chapter 12

BLESSINGS OVERLOOKED

Many everyday blessings are commonly over-looked. Have you ever thanked God for the earth upon which we live? The folks in Enterprise, Alabama, sure did when they began to see their peanut crop explode with profit. Think about all the earth provides to sustain us: food, water, minerals, oil—the list is quite long. Yes, somebody was in-volved in the process with blood, sweat, and tears. But their efforts alone would be useless without the added blessing of God.

One day, a depressed man stopped by my office. He told me there was nothing he could be thankful for. So I asked, "Would you like to go with me as I make my hospital visits?"

He agreed when I promised we'd stop for a morning coffee break with a donut. I didn't say much to him as we made our rounds. We stopped by the bedside of a lady in her mid 40s who was dying of cancer; we visited a man with heart disease who was waiting for a heart transplant; we saw a very sharp young man who was dying of AIDS; we chatted with a lady in her 60s who was recovering from a hip replacement; and we ended with a visit to the nursery to check on a baby born with a cleft palate. It was a typical day of hospital visits for a pastor.

When we finally sat down with our donuts and coffee, he asked, "Is it like this every day you visit the hospital?"

"Yes, pretty much like this—different people, all with different problems," I replied.

There was a pregnant moment of silence...then he said, "I don't think I'll grumble again about my situation, at least not for a while."

What about your "SPECIAL BLESSINGS"? What special blessings? Yes, you have had them and I have had them at some point in the past. You may not have recognized them as such at the time, but that's what they were.

A woman prepared to receive her 85-year-old mother back home after the mother had been in a nursing home. One month prior to the event, she and her husband were blessed with four weeks at a luxurious beach house. Nothing could have meant more to her, for she loved the beach. Little did she know what difficulties would lie ahead. The older woman suffered heart failure and was put on oxygen. The next three weeks were extremely difficult for her as she cared for her dying mother. But through it all, she was grateful for God's goodness in giving them the time at the beach as a blessing to remember.

God never bestows blessings just for an hour or two. It's a special pledge; it's as though God is saying, "I'll do this for you now so that you will always know that you are the object of My love."

It's a sad thing that we forget so quickly. One of the reasons why new problems and unexpected dangers can startle us with fear is because we have forgotten past mercies. We can be calm and collected in the face of new troubles if we bring to mind how God has helped and sustained us! With such precious memories we can face the future and say, "The God who delivered me then is the same God who will deliver me now!"

Let's make it a practice of remembering all the special blessings that come our way. But let's not just make it a practice of thanking God for His blessings, but also those people who were involved in bringing us blessings. It's amazing what this can and will do for others as well as for your own spiritual well-being. It's also pleasing to God. Often, He sends some of His special mercies by the hands of other people. In fact, He normally does. And He likes for his "special agent" to be thanked, too.

HAVE WE IGNORED THE "GREATEST" BLESSING? We have been reminded of the common blessings often overlooked, the special blessings too soon forgotten...but what of the "greatest" blessing of all?

What is this "greatest" blessing? The Apostle Paul brings it into focus: "Thanks be to God for his indescribable gift!" (II Corinthians 9:15) The word "indescribable" means simply that it's impossible to put it into words. What is this gift? This indescribable gift is Jesus Christ! Thanks be to God, above everything else, so says Paul, for Him. Do we say the same thing? What would your life be like without Jesus Christ?

Consider what Baron von Hugel wrote concerning this subject: "I should not be physically alive at this moment; I should be, were I alive at all, a corrupt or at least an incredibly unhappy, violent, bitter, self-occupied destructive soul, were it not for Jesus Christ and for having come and saved me from myself...it, and nothing else."

(II Corinthians 9:15)

⚡ POWER POINT: Take a little time and trouble to thank someone who has blessed you. Send a note, give a call, or visit them one day and let them know what the blessing has meant to you.

Chapter 13

IT'S INVENTORY TIME

What if God were to take His Word and condense it down to a single message for your life, what would it be? I suppose that would be a bit presumptuous on my part to claim to have the entire answer to that question; however, I'll share a few thoughts with you.

You, yes, you are one of God's greatest miracles; therefore, it's time to count your blessings! God has already sent prophets, poets, wise men, artists, composers, writers, and preachers with a word about your potential. You have been told that YOU are the salt of the earth, YOU are the light of this world, YOU have the secret of mountain-moving faith! Too many of us have used our average intelligence, personal handicaps, lack of opportunity, or past failures as an excuse for our present state of ineffectiveness. And when all else has failed, we have blamed God!

Let's make a decision to change our perspective on life and begin to take a "blessing" inventory.

Are you blind? Most of us can see quite well with the 100 million receptors God has placed in our eyes. This has enabled us to enjoy the magic of snowflakes floating down toward earth, the beauty of a spring flower emerging from beneath the cold ground, the majesty of an eagle in flight...clouds, stars, rainbows...the look of love! Count one huge blessing!

Are you deaf? Most of us can hear with the 24,000 fibers God has built into each of our ears to vibrate to the wind in the trees, tides on the rocks, an orchestra in concert, a robin's morning song, children's joyous laughter at play, and the words, "I love you." Count another blessing!

Are you mute? Most of us can talk, unlike any of God's other creatures, and our words can calm the angry, lift the depressed, goad the quitter, cheer the unhappy, warm the lonely, praise the worthy, encourage the defeated, teach the ignorant, and say, "I love you." Count some more!

Are you paralyzed? Most of us can move. We aren't a tree condemned to one small plot of ground; we can run, climb, and dance. God has designed all of our 500 muscles, 200 bones, and seven miles of nerve fibers to be synchronized to do our bidding. Are you still counting?

Is your skin diseased? Do people turn in horror when you approach? Most of us can say no to this also! Our skin is clear and a marvel of creation. It only requires that we clean it and care for it. In time, all steel will rust but not your skin. The strongest metal will eventually wear out but not your skin! It constantly renews itself; old cells are replaced by the new. Count another blessing!

Are your lungs befouled? Do you struggle to breathe? Most of us can say no! Our "portholes to life" support us even in the vilest of environments; they labor continually to filter life-giving oxygen through some six million pockets of folded flesh while they rid our body of gaseous wastes. Count this blessing!

Is your heart stricken? Does it leak and strain to maintain your life? Most of us can say no! Our heart is strong. Touch your chest and feel its rhythm, pulsating hour after hour, 36 million beats each year, asleep or awake, pumping your blood through more than 60,000 miles of veins, arteries, and tubing. It pumps more than 600,000 gallons per year. Such a wonderful pump has never been created by science. Count a big blessing!

Is your blood poisoned? Within your five quarts of blood are more than 22 trillion blood cells; and in each cell are millions of molecules; and inside each molecule is an atom oscillating at more than 10 million times per second. Each second, two million of your blood cells die to be replaced by two million more in a resurrection that has continued since your birth. Count more blessings!

You may not be able to say that every one of these blessings are yours right now. But chances are the majority of them are blessings you can count on. So count every one of them and know that you are one of God's greatest miracles! Know that one of the major secrets to happiness and success is that you already possess every blessing necessary to achieve great glory! No wonder the Psalmist wrote:

> I praise You because I am fearfully
>   and wonderfully made;
> Your works are wonderful,
> I know that full well.
> My frame was not hidden from you when
>   I was made in the secret place.
> When I was woven together in the depths of the
>   earth,
> Your eyes saw my unformed body.
> All the days ordained for me
> Were written in your book
> Before one of them came to be!
>   *(Psalm 139:14-16)*

⚡ POWER POINT: Next time you visit the doctor's office, give thanks for the health you have enjoyed and the many wonderful functions of your body.

Chapter 14

MORE INVENTORY TIME

There really is no way we will be able to exhaust the things for which we are or should be giving thanks! But let's continue...

Are you feeble of mind? Did you know that your brain is the most complex structure in the universe? Within its three pounds are more than 13 billion nerve cells! These help you file away every perception, every sound, every taste, every smell, every action you have experienced! God has implanted within these brain cells more than 1,000 billion-billion protein molecules. Every single incident of your life is there, most of them waiting your instant recall.

To assist your brain in the control of your body, God has dispersed throughout your body four million pain-sensitive structures, 500,000 touch detectors, and more than 200,000 temperature detectors! No nation's gold supply is better protected than you are. None of our ancient or modern wonders are greater than you! Count another blessing!

Are you rare and unique? Absolutely! You are not one of the herd! You are not headed for mediocrity. YOU are valuable because God created only one of you! You arrived bringing with you, as does every child, the promise that God is not yet finished with mankind! Two cells united in a miracle, each containing 23 chromosomes and within each chromosome hundreds of genes that govern every characteristic about you. With all the possible combinations at God's command, beginning with that single sperm from your father's more than 400 million, through the hundreds of genes in each of the chromosomes of your father and mother, God could have created 300,000 billion humans, each different from the other! But who did God bring forth? YOU! You are one of a kind, rarest of the rare, a priceless treasure possessed of qualities in mind, speech, movement, appearance, and actions like no other who has ever lived, now lives, or shall live! Count many more blessings!

Are you poor? Not hardly! You are rich, wealthy beyond calculation! We have just tallied up some of your assets. Count them again! How much is life worth? How much is health worth? How much is your physical body worth? How much is the ability to feel, touch, hear, and taste worth? Why do you deceive yourself into believing that you are powerless to change your life? Are you without talents, senses, abilities, pleasures, instincts, sensations, and dignity? Are you without hope? Of course not. Count many more blessings!

And then...the greatest human need—are you loved? Yes! God loves you with an everlasting, eternal love. Love is a gift for which no return is demanded. Love not returned is not lost, for love not reciprocated by another will flow back to you from someone else to soften and purify your heart. Count another blessing...in fact, count twice more!

Absolutely awesome! Don't ever say, "There's nothing for which I can give thanks!" You and I have so much! Our blessings overflow our capacity to contain them; our ability to express thanks seems so small in comparison. What rich person—old, sick, feeble, and helpless—wouldn't exchange all the gold in their vault for these blessings which we have taken for granted?

THEREFORE...wipe away your tears, reach out and grasp the hand of God, stand up straight, and offer thanksgiving!

The Psalmist continues with his expression of praise...

How precious to me are your thoughts, O God!
How vast is the sum of them!
Were I to count them,
They would outnumber the grains of sand!
(Psalm 139:17-18)

POWER POINT: What specific things about your mind and emotions can you especially give thanks for?

Chapter 15

AFFIRMATIONS

An "affirmation" is a statement of positive force. It's always worded in the present and usually begins with the words, "I am" or "I can." When you make affirmations, you are making firm, positive statements about yourself. This action is more than simply acknowledging parts of your "inventory" as we did in the last two chapters.

Although affirmations may be a more accurate description of the future than the present, the fulfillment of the affirmation is always stated in the present. Affirmations can be said anywhere, silently or out loud. The more often they're used, the more they truly become a part of you.

Why talk about affirmations when we have been dealing with thanksgiving? Simple. This is a positive method by which you can begin to cultivate the attitude of gratitude. This is a "how-to-do-it" session.

Is this a biblical concept? Absolutely! Here is a very short sampling of some of the affirmations you can find in God's Word:

"I can do everything through him who gives me strength" (Philippians 4:13).

"I am glad and rejoice with all of you" (Philippians 2:17b).

"I know whom I have believed, and am convinced that he is able to guard what I have entrusted to him for that day" (II Timothy 2:12).

"I have fought the good fight, I have finished the race, I have kept the faith" (II Timothy 4:7).

In order for an affirmation to begin to work in your life, picture it on the video screen of your mind. See yourself living it out in real life.

Affirmations become more powerful as you repeat them. Write them down, place a copy on the dash of your car, over the shaving mirror, etc. You may well experience all kinds of negative thoughts and feelings that will pop to the surface to keep you from fulfilling the affirmation. Let them surface in your mind and allow them to float away. Beneath all that garbage, there is a part of you that knows the truth of what you are affirming.

Create your own affirmations to suit your situation. Keep them positive statements of the present. "*I am* grateful," not "*I want to be* grateful."

How about affirmations to help you cultivate an attitude of gratitude in all situations:

"I am grateful for the life God has given me."

"I am free to express my gratitude to God as well as to others."

"I constantly find things, big and small, for which I can express my thanks."

"I set my heart to joyfully and automatically focus on the good, the virtuous, and the positive in others."

"I rejoice in the Lord all day long."

The battle for your soul is in the mind, and the victory must be won there. If you have nurtured a negative and ungrateful attitude, it may take some time before the affirmations take effect. You see, it's not just changing an attitude; it's changing an attitude which will, in turn, allow you to change your actions. You will become a grateful person, which will enable you to experience more contentment than you could have dreamed possible.

(Philippians 4:13, 2:17; II Timothy 2:12, 4:7; Psalm 39:1, 42:11)

⚡ POWER POINT: Let me challenge you to a Bible study in which you search for all the "affirmations" in the Word! As you find them, begin using them in your daily life and see what a difference it makes!

Chapter 16

WHAT IS IT ALL ABOUT?

Ours is the most affluent era in the history of the world! This generation has grown up in a time economic depression is virtually unknown. We've always had plenty, and it's been easy for us to take it all for granted. Many seem to feel that the world owes them not only a living but luxuries which were unheard of a short 50 years ago. Too often those who receive the most, appreciate it the least. We have become all too ready to bite the hand that has fed us. This is true of nations, families, and individuals.

Alben Barkley, former Vice-President of the United States, visited a small town in his district when he was a congressman. He crossed the street to shake hands with a person whom he had befriended in the past and asked, "Jeb, are you going to vote for me in this upcoming election?"

"No, sir," was the taciturn reply.

"Why not? Didn't I help your wife get special

medical care when she was sick? Didn't I find that job your daughter is working at? Didn't I help you get a loan when you bought your farm?" questioned Mr. Barkley.

"Well, yes, you did all those things," he paused, then continued, "but you ain't done nothing for me *lately*."

Selfishness is ugly in all forms, especially when it's mixed with prideful ego. Henry Ward Beecher reminds us that "pride always slays thanksgiving, but a humble mind is the soil out of which thanks naturally grows. A proud man is seldom a grateful man, for he never thinks that he gets as much as he deserves."

Ingratitude toward a fellow human being is bad enough, but ingratitude toward God is without excuse. Paul listed ingratitude toward God among some of the worst sins of mankind: "For although they knew God, they neither glorified him as God nor gave thanks to him, but their thinking became futile and their foolish hearts were darkened" (Romans 1:21). In our society we are facing the same thanklessness. Where are the folks who glorify God today? Look everywhere about you, and you'll see a great number who are not giving thanks. They are more concerned about enjoying creature comforts than with fulfilling the Creator's purpose for their life.

We need to be, as the Apostle Paul says, "always

giving thanks to God the Father for everything in the name of our Lord Jesus Christ" (Ephesians 5:20). There is a very strong statement in the original Greek: "always giving thanks." It translates as "having the habit of giving thanks always." Yes, the giving of thanks is a habit and it's also an art. It is something which must be both acquired and cultivated! It's a personal discipline!

A baby is not born with a thankful spirit! There is nothing more selfish than an infant. Its entire world centers on itself. A baby takes and takes all that we give and still cries for more. As the baby grows older, he/she develops an awareness of other people. But even then, this little person must be taught to share, to be appreciative, and to express thanks.

How many times have you given something to a child and then heard the mother say, "Now, what do you say to the nice person?" If the quick reply is a thank you, you know that the child is being taught the art. The real tragedy is that too many people grow in age and stature but remain babies in the art of thanksgiving.

Shakespeare said: "How sharper than a serpent's tooth it is to have a thankless child."

John Milton spoke of such people when he penned the following lines:

Swinish gluttony, Ne'er looks to heav'n
Amidst his gorgeous feast,

But with besotted base ingratitude
Crams, and blasphemes his feeder.

A person's maturity in human graces can be measured by their degree of appreciation for the kindness of others.

Samuel Johnson wrote: "Gratitude is the fruit of great cultivation; you do not find it among gross people."

GRATITUDE, therefore, may be considered one of the primary marks of greatness!

(Romans 1:21; Ephesians 5:20)

⚡ POWER POINT: Instead of making a list of all the things you want for Christmas, why not have everyone in your family make a list of all their material blessings. The night before Christmas, gather everyone together and read them aloud.

Chapter 17

THE OBJECT OF THANKSGIVING

It's one thing to say "thanks" to another person when you are given a gift, an act of kindness, or a comforting word. But it is another to express gratitude to God who is the fountain from which flows all good things. If giving thanks to one another is an admirable quality, then giving thanks to God is an expression of nobility. It is a recognition that "every good and perfect gift is from above..." (James 1:17).

It's on this precise point that the sin of ingratitude can be germinated. In our complex, urban life, most of us get our milk and veggies from grocery store shelves. We miss seeing the seed sown into the ground, the fertile soil, and the part that sun and rain play in the growth of the fruit of the field. We hardly ever see the cows grazing in the pasture. Our needs are supplied so mechanically that we fail to remember the part God and the farmer play in it. The farther we get from the soil, the more hardened we become to Him who supplies these needs. We become like a hog who gorges on its food, yet never lifts its snout toward heaven in thanks…never questioning where the supply of food has come from.

If a thankless child is a burden to parents, think how much more so is a thankless person to God. When Jesus healed the 10 lepers, only one returned to express thanks. The pathos of the heart of God is felt in the poignant question Jesus asked, "Where are the other nine?" (Luke 17:17) Where, indeed?

Mankind's communication with God is called prayer, and the highest point in prayer is the giving of thanks and praise to God. Therefore, let us rise to these heights of communion with God as we "enter his gates with thanksgiving and his courts with praise; give thanks to him and praise his name" (Psalm 100:4).

It's not so important what happens to you but how you react to it that really matters. Jerome K. Jerome said that "in every cloud is an angel's face." The tough things we encounter provide the opportunity for us to mature. Further, E. H. Chapin reminds us that, "Tribulation will not hurt you unless it hardens you and makes you sour, narrow, and skeptical." If you endure these tests through the power of God, expressing your thanks as you make it through…the angel's face will eventually come shining through!

God does not will your misfortunes! In His

wisdom, however, He may not remove them quickly. Through them all, He may be saying to you, "My grace is sufficient for you..." (II Corinthians 12:9). Eventually, you may come to the point, as did the great apostle, where you can say, "I delight in weaknesses, in insults, in hardships, in persecutions, in difficulties. For when I am weak, then I am strong" (II Corinthians 12:10).

This way of life is not only for a chosen few! It is for all who are willing to confront every challenge in their lives with praise and thanksgiving.

Yes, you *can* and *should* be thankful! Thank God for His goodness toward you: your life, your family, your health, your strength, your work, your opportunity to glorify Him! If trouble is your lot, thank God for His sustaining grace through it all. When you are tempted to complain, simply count your blessings, and you will find that have no time for complaint!

The Rev. Hershel Hobbs recounts the following: "It was almost 30 years ago that I first met her. She was living in a nursing home. Due to ill health she could never leave her room. Most of her time was spent in bed. In her every waking moment, her body was filled with pain. As her pastor, I visited her often. Never did I hear her complain. I went to bring her a blessing, but I always carried away a greater one.

"I do not remember her name, but I shall never forget her smile. You see, she never used her name.

She called herself, 'The Sunshine Lady.' Though she never left her room, through all these years she has scattered sunshine abroad even beyond our city. Here is how she does it. Out of her meager income, she purchases beautiful cards and stamps. Daily she searches the newspapers for names and events. If someone received a blessing, say the birth of a baby, she writes to rejoice with them. Or if someone has experienced a sorrow, she writes words of sympathy and strength. Only recently a friend in another city sent me such a letter that she had received. As always it was signed, 'The Sunshine lady!'"

(Luke 17:17; Psalm 100:4; II Corinthians 12:9-10)

POWER POINT: Buy a pack of thank-you notes and see if you can use them all up in one week!

Chapter 18

THE EVERYTHING ATTITUDE

Hopefully you have begun to increasingly focus on the positive things in your life. We discussed in chapter two that we must be thankful IN everything. In the previous chapter, we hinted at how to take thanksgiving a step further: We must learn to be grateful FOR everything in our life! You might be thinking, "That's not possible!"

The following progressive plan will help you begin the process. The first step is to start with giving thanks for the outstanding things, then move to the more common things, next to the not-so-good things, then to the very not-so-good, and finally, tackle the downright horrible things!

Yes, I know, it sounds so simple when written down like this. The question again surfaces, "Why should we be grateful for the tough things, the really terrible things we sometimes experience in life?" To begin with, an attitude of gratitude pays fantastic dividends. It makes you stronger so that when you're faced with difficult circumstances, you've already been fortified for the battle and have the inner strength to persevere.

Why are difficult situations a part of human experience? It's very likely we may never entirely understand why God allows challenges to be part of our life. However, if we're steadfast with maintaining a correct attitude, we'll come to a new understanding that *the things which almost break us are in reality the things which make us*.

Negative thinking cannot exist where there is a wonderful consciousness of gratitude. Nasty thoughts may surface, but an attitude of thankfulness responds, "Thank you for that thought. I understand now what *not* to be thinking. Because of the grace of God, I will endeavor to do/think/accomplish the opposite." What you've just done is to replace the negative with a positive. You can't simply tell that nasty thought to go away. It *must be replaced* by something more powerful.

There are lots of things in everyday life that we could complain about, but there's so much more to be thankful for. Where should we start? Take your pick. Try this: in the middle of your next power outage, think of everything you can be grateful for: God who put coal in the ground, which is burned to generate electricity; Edison for inventing the light bulb; the power company for providing electricity to your home; the artist who designed the lamp; or the electrician for his skilled work. Do this instead of griping at the inconvenience of being without electricity, and see what a difference it makes!

Expressing gratitude is a powerful factor in healthy, fabulous living. It's an attitude which sets you free to really live. That's why I'm strongly suggesting you look for things to be grateful about—not so the electric company will receive thank-you notes (although wouldn't that be refreshing to the employee who opened the mail), but so you'll know the joy and excitement of being grateful!

There is a law written somewhere in the universe by the God who created it that goes something like this: LET'S GIVE MORE TO THE GRATEFUL BECAUSE THEY ARE GRATEFUL!

(I Thessalonians 5:18)

⚡ POWER POINT: How about throwing a "gratitude party?" Invite yourself and then bring people from your past and present into the sanctuary of your mind and, one at a time, thank them for the contributions they have made to your life. Who should they be? How about parents, siblings, spouse, teachers, friends, pastors, bosses, business associates, children, and on and on. Picture them, one at a time under your glowing light of appreciation. Express your thanks...then consider the possibility of inviting them to actually get together and do it in person.

Chapter 19

BE A BLESSING

We've spent lots of time on what, why, how, and when to express our gratitude for things done to us or for us. However, there is another side to the coin of thanks—it's being a blessing to someone else so that, in turn, they might have something for which to express their gratitude.

I know of a person who when asked about life goals will always reply that her only goal in life is simply, "To be a blessing!" Now this idea can be a bit frustrating to people who develop action plans, goals, and benchmarks by which to measure their progress. What kind of a goal is this?

Think about it. "To be a blessing" is, in reality, a profound goal. Let's look at this scenario: You have just signed a contract to render a service or provide a product for a company or person in return for their money. What if, unknowingly, because of an error or omission, they are unable to pay you? So what will you do? Will you immediately sue them? Or will you carefully consider how you can still be a blessing to them, for example, by cancelling the contract, extending payments, or working out some other way for them to overcome their financial difficulties?

What if, on the other hand, you are the one whose circumstances change and you are unable to pay the amount you owe someone? What will you do? Will you be like the man in Psalms 15 who "keeps his oath even when it hurts?"

"Wait a minute," you say. "Sounds like I'm always getting the short end of the stick." Not really. You are always getting the opportunity to live a godly life that will bring great blessing to you and to those around you. It says of that man in Psalms 15, "He who does these things will never be shaken." In this day of heightened anxiety, wouldn't it be great to "never be shaken?"

The Book of Proverbs is full of life principles, especially when it comes to gaining wisdom. "Do not withhold good from those who deserve it, when it is in your power to act" (Proverbs 3:27). Now that is life-changing! When you have the power to act, be a blessing and don't procrastinate about it! Talk about wisdom for today's work world! What kind of a world would this be if everybody made it their life focus to be a blessing?

When you look at the results of the ministry of Jesus on this earth, you will discover that plants bloomed, people were healed and even restored to life, relationships and attitudes were transformed, lifestyles were turned around, and eternal destinies were changed!

Yes, I know there were some notable exceptions such as the fig tree which He cursed, the Pharisees whom He declared to be whited sepulchers, the religious leaders who had a vested interest in seeing Him destroyed, and even Judas who betrayed Him. But what did He say His life mission was? He stated that he came "to preach good news to the poor...to proclaim freedom for the prisoners and recovery of sight for the blind, to release the oppressed, to proclaim the year of the Lord's favor" (Luke 4:18-19). In others words, He came to be a blessing to all in need *who would accept Him.*

The Bible contains numerous pictures of what blessings look like: rivers flowing in the deserts, lions laying down with lambs, hungry people being fed, wedding parties becoming more joyful, good news being shared, people being restored to health, and much more.

Did these blessings bring happiness and joy to the recipients? You know it! Did all of them respond with gratitude? NO! But that was not His responsibility, and neither is it yours. We are to be a blessing; what others do with it or how they respond to what they have received is *their* responsibility. Did all of them return to express their thanks to God or to Jesus Christ? NO! This is a common problem we see repeated again and again. Instead of being grateful, many of them only wanted more. Again, not your problem. Our assignment is to be a blessing!

Another observation of the human condition is that when something bad happens, people's first reaction curse others. How many "blessing" words do we know and how often do we use them?

Jesus came to bless, not curse! To heal, not burden! To bring life, not death! To bring abundance, not lack! To make the crooked places straight, not build barriers! To wipe away tears, not bring sorrow! To be a blessing!

What about you?

(Genesis 3:9; Proverbs 3:27; Luke 4:18-19)

⚡ POWER POINT: Try to be a blessing to someone at work this week in a way you've never been before.

Chapter 20

JUST SAY "THANKS!"

Golfing great Jack Nicklaus is legendary for saying "thanks." Back in the early days of his budding career, he stayed in private homes during tournaments because he couldn't afford motels or hotels. He always wrote a thank-you note to those who had shown him hospitality. Even after he became a superstar both in the world of golf and business, Nicklaus still looked for ways to express his gratitude to others. Early in life, he had evidently learned the principle that Bob Briner writes about: "In business, really in all of life, it is impossible to say 'thank you' too many times!"

Do people ever get tired of hearing you say "thanks" to them? Not hardly. It's a small courtesy which pays off in rich rewards.

Throughout the gospels, we see Jesus' example of showing gratitude to others and to His Father. He showed appreciation for the love demonstrated by the woman who bathed his feet with tears. He thanked His Father for always hearing Him when

He prayed. As He departed for heaven, He gave thanks for the followers who were left behind and the work they would be doing.

When Jesus established the Church, the organization which was to continue the work He had been sent to do, He emphasized servanthood. His way is in direct contrast to the short-term, get-rich-quick business style of our world, which is to only take care of #1 (and of course *we* are #1), with no appreciation for what others have done for you. The bottom-line reality is that the surest way for long-term success in the business world is to learn to put the customer and the employee first, never forgetting to say thanks along the way. Yet so few are willing to learn this simple concept from the lifestyle of Jesus.

Expressing gratitude to others doesn't mean that you roll over and become a wimp. Not at all. It is a strong, positive approach to life and business. It's a tough-minded stance. Take good care of your employees and your customers, showing them gratefulness for all that they do, and they will take care of you. Is it biblical? Read Matthew 23:11: "The greatest among you will be your servant. For whoever exalts himself will be humbled and whoever humbles himself will be exalted." Expressing gratitude keeps you humble, for you admit that you couldn't have done it all yourself; and that others, in fact, made a significant contribution to your success.

This is a principle upon which any business or life can be built successfully!

There's an old Jewish story about a rabbi who prayed: "O Lord, make me holy! Make me like Moses!"

The rabbi paused. Then he heard God reply, "What need have I of another Moses? I already have one! But what I really could use is YOU!"

What a profound truth. God has no need for clones, not even clones of His greatest saints. God needs originals, one-of-a-kind-ers—YOU and ME! People who have learned how to give thanks as an act of servanthood. It's when we are ourselves, shaped in His image, doing what has been asked of us, that we bring the most glory and joy to God and to others.

Comic strip "Lucy" is down in the dumps and says to Linus, "My life is a drag. I've never been so low in all my life."

Linus, the great encourager, tries to cheer her up by saying, "When you're in a mood like this you should think of the things you have to be thankful for, count your blessings."

Lucy replies, "That's a good one. What do I have to be thankful for?"

"Well, for one thing," Linus says, "you have a brother who loves you."

Lucy responds, "Sometimes, you say the right things."

Now...let's say the right things, beginning with "thanks!"

(Matthew 23:11)

POWER POINT: This week write down every time you say thanks to someone. At the end of the week, add it up and think how you could increase your total.

Chapter 21

THANKSGIVING ALL YEAR LONG

There is a famous painting you may have seen of cattle feeding at a trough with this inscription on it:

Who without prayer sits down to eat,
And without thanks then leaves the table,
Tramples the gift of God with feet,
And is like the mule and ox in the stable.
(*Author unknown*)

Thanksgiving is a grace. The original root term used is *charis* meaning "the grace of God." It's something that operates in the soul of the believer as a principle and returns to God. The gratitude of those who walk with the Lord connects every good gift and every perfect gift with God. *The Christian privilege and responsibility is to find reason for gratitude in all things.* We are to be "always giving thanks to God the Father for everything in the name of our Lord Jesus Christ" (Ephesians 5:20).

Let's take a look at a few more things for which we can express thanks:

The gift of freedom: We have sung the following words so often but perhaps without any thought of gratitude:

"My Country, 'tis of Thee,
Sweet land of liberty, of Thee I sing."

Freedom…purchased for all of us at such a great price! Think of what it really means to be free. Our nation is the envy of the rest of the world. We have the freedom to worship, to love, to vote, to make our own mistakes, and many more.

The gift of the field: Food…do you realize that when we go to sleep tonight, more than a third of the world's population is still hungry?

Consider what an agricultural college found in a study: in the production of 200 bushels of corn on one acre of land, the following materials are used: 4,000,000 pounds of water; 6,800 pounds of oxygen; 5,200 pounds of carbon; 160 pounds of nitrogen; 125 pounds of potassium, 40 pounds of magnesium; 50 pounds of calcium, two pounds of iron; and smaller amounts of iodine, zinc and copper! Who must we thank for our food?

The gift of beauty: Line, texture, symmetry, and grace are all aspects of beauty. Beauty can found in a sunset, in an apple, a spider web, clouds, mountains, water, or the Grand Canyon. Rarely are man-made things of such lasting beauty.

The gift of choice: God has given us a free will. Consider that through the exercise of this gift there are a multitude of possibilities open to us. You are free to make choices every day of your life which affect your future.

The gift of life: Life is vitally precious. In fact, the urge to live is the strongest of all human drives. It is truly a priceless gift, whether it is long or short. Each of us can look over the past and think of people whom we know and have loved who are missing in our circles and realize what a gift their life was to us.

The following is a letter to the editor that appeared in the Chicago Tribune:

"I am not a writer, but I am taking some space in the newspaper to write something special about Kathy. We weren't so special, you know, I'm just a little insurance man, but when someone makes your life so good, you just hate to let her leave the world without some kind of memorial to let people know she was alive. I want to tell people to look over at their husbands and wives and say to themselves, 'My

God, look what I have here!' People take so much for granted. It's as if they think everyone is going to live forever and they can put off their love and appreciation until they have time.

"Here I am saying these things about Kathy today, and it seems like I never said them to her when she was alive. She'd have come to me now with kisses. I am sitting home alone at night, and I see her in the hallways. I see the furniture we bought, and I see her sitting beside me on the couch. If I could go back again, I would do everything different. I would let her know how much she meant to me, but I can't do that and it seems like the only thing I can do is try to make other people know it. Look at your husband. Look at your wife. Look at your kids. Look at your friends. If you think you have things pretty nice, say it out loud! Don't assume that they are going to be there forever. Some day they are going to walk out the door and never come back again. I didn't think of that until Kathy was dead. It's too late for me, but it's not too late for YOU!"

(Ephesians 5:20)

 POWER POINT: This week try to follow the advice above and see what a difference it makes!

Chapter 22
TO ALL YE PILGRIMS

The story of the very first Thanksgiving celebration in our country is familiar to all of us. But to fully appreciate it, we must recall all the events that took place prior to that feast. The Pilgrims sailed across the Atlantic Ocean on the Mayflower and landed at Plymouth Rock in December of 1620. They managed to stretch the provisions they had brought with them to get them through their first harsh New England winter.

The next summer, they planted a communal garden, but these settlers didn't know how to plant Indian corn and so the crop was meager. In November, 1621, more pilgrims arrived without adequate provisions. Governor William Bradford was worried when he calculated that the food provisions would only last six more months at half rations per person.

After the second hard winter, another ship arrived in May, 1622, with seven more pilgrims and some letters...but no food! The food supply was almost gone, and the early settlers were starving. Shortly thereafter, another ship arrived which brought a small amount of provisions, but each settler's ration was still down to a quarter of a pound of bread per day. Because of their hunger, some of them stole food from the communal garden and had to be punished. So in early 1623, the settlers decided to parcel out the land to individual families and let all families tend their personal crops. Governor Bradford wrote that everyone worked harder under this plan.

In his own words: "The women now wente willing into ye field, and took their little ones with them to set corne, which before would aledge weakness, and disabilities; whom to have compelled would have been through great tiranie and oppression."

After planting their crops that year, the Pilgrims were deeply concerned whether they would grow. Governor Bradford noted that all the families really meant it when they prayed, "Lord, give us this day our daily bread." When the next ship arrived that summer, the passengers were shocked and frightened by the look of the starving settlers.

But by harvest time, their private gardens were a huge success! In a spirit of deep gratitude toward God, Governor Bradford declared a day of thanksgiving. In the years to come, harvests became even more plentiful, but the pilgrims continued to put five kernels of corn beside their dinner plates when they celebrated Thanksgiving to remind them of the great suffering and starvation endured by the first settlers.

The following is the text of Governor Bradford's Thanksgiving declaration:

Inasmuch as the Great Father has given us this year an abundant harvest of Indian corne, wheat, beans, squashes, and garden vegetables, and has made the forests to abound with game and the sea with fish and clams,

And inasmuch as He has protected us from the ravages of the savages,

Has spared us from pestilence and disease,

Has granted us freedom to worship God according to the dictates of our own conscience;

Now, I, your magistrate,

DO PROCLAIM THAT ALL YE PILGRIMS, With your wives and little ones,

Do gather at ye meeting house, on ye hill, between the hours of nine and twelve in the day time, on Thursday, November ye 29th of the year of our Lord one thousand six hundred and twenty-three,

And the third year since ye Pilgrims landed on ye Pilgrim Rock,

There to listen to ye pastor,

And render THANKSGIVING to ye Almighty God for all His blessings."
　　　　　　—William Bradford,
　　　　　　Ye Governor of ye Colony

(Psalm 1:1-3)

⚡ POWER POINT: This Thanksgiving, why not have all your guests come ready to share one thing for which they would like to give thanks.

Chapter 23

BALANCE

When your life is in balance, with thanksgiving undergirding it, you will find that it gives you a spiritual attitude toward life which lifts you above your environment. Gratitude doesn't depend on *where* you live or *what* you have, but it does depend upon *who* you are.

If the spirit of thanksgiving depended upon physical or material well-being, our American celebration surely wouldn't have begun in the Plymouth Colony in New England. Even though they had experienced one good harvest, life in the colony was still full of many difficult hardships. No, an attitude of thanksgiving in all circumstances has more to do with your spiritual condition. When your life is lived in an attitude of gratefulness, balanced with all the other needs, you will experience a peace which passes all understanding.

The Greek philosopher, Cicero, captured the essence of this attitude when he said: "A thankful heart is not only the greatest virtue, but the parent of all the other virtues."

Have you noticed some contradictions in this book? Well, so have I. Welcome to the real world, for life is sometimes like a balancing act. For example, should we work on our attitude or just force ourselves to thank others? Should we take some time to contemplate about our lot in life in order to change it or just be grateful and content with where we are? Should we be assertive or accepting? Giving or receiving? Thinking or doing?

There is no easy answer to any of these questions. You see, it's a matter of timing and the seasons of life in which you find yourself. Thanksgiving is always necessary; it's just the outworking of it in our lives that's in question. How does God want us to live? It's a matter of balance!

Okay…how is it possible to find that "just right" balance? Balance is a point between the extremes. And yet, to complicate things, the point is always shifting, always moving, depending upon our level of maturity. A successful life can be much like a successful tightrope walk. There are times when the balance pole dips one way, perhaps toward contentment and being at peace; and sometimes it dips gently to the other, toward actively seeking how to bless others. Then there are times when it's perfectly still and you know that for the time being you have things in balance.

How does one find and maintain balance? Vigilance! Internal, constant vigilance that seeks to weigh our thoughts and actions and see if they measure up to what we have been called to be and do. This is the price of balance, the price of freedom in living.

When you notice an "out-of-balance" situation in your lifestyle, attempt to balance it immediately! Tip the pole in the other direction by changing your attitude internally and watch things change in your life externally.

To find the exact point of balance, ask yourself the question which has become so popular today: "What would Jesus do?" Look at your life's situation through the eyes of the Master. Concerning our subject—thanksgiving—Jesus often expressed His thanks to His heavenly Father. He took the time to commend the only leper out of the 10 who had been healed for coming back to offer thanks. "Where are the others?" He asked. WWJD? Sometimes He would do quite a lot…at other times He did little or nothing. Thinking about what He would do, helps you to consider what your actions should be.

When finding your point of balance for all the positive things which should mark your life, keep in mind that thankfulness is one of those foundational stones upon which the rest of your life will be built. It's an attitude which undergirds everything else.

Peter Lathan wrote: "Fortunate, indeed, is the

man who takes exactly the right measure of himself, and holds a just balance between what he can acquire and what he can use, be it great or small."

It's foundational to living a full, well-rounded lifestyle. Thanksgiving was never intended to be confined to a season or day, it must become a balanced lifestyle which brings honor and glory to the God whom we serve and is a joy to others who are part of our circle of relationships!